Becoming Me Again

A FAITH-BASED JOURNEY OF WEIGH LOSS, DISCIPLINE AND HEALING

WENOMIA GOODRUM

In loving memory of my Uncle Johnny.
"Just you and me, kid."
You saw me before I saw myself again.
Your love lit the road back home to me.

"Sometimes the journey back to yourself begins with the courage to admit you've been gone." —

Wenomia Goodrum

Acknowledgements

To everyone who loved me when I didn't recognize the woman in the mirror... thank you.

Courtney — The heartbeat I carry everywhere I go.

Char – You inspire me more than you will ever know.

Anita – You are "That Girl". One who is always there.

Phyllis – My prayer partner, my encourager.

To my family — For being my roots and my wings.

And to every person on a journey back to themselves... you are worthy of coming home.

Contents

Becoming Me Again

A Faith-Based Journey of Weigh Loss, Discipline and Healing

Wenomia Goodrum

Introduction

For years, I carried weight that didn't belong to me. Some of it was physical, but most of it was invisible — emotional burdens, unmet needs, heartbreaks I never voiced, responsibilities I never put down.

Somewhere along the way, as I showed up for everyone else, I disappeared inside my own life.

The day I looked at myself and didn't recognize the woman staring back at me was the day everything shifted. Her eyes were tired. Her spirit dimmed. Her body heavy — not just from weight, but from years of emotional load.

I didn't just want to lose weight.

I wanted to find me again.

My journey began not with perfection, but with honesty.

Small steps.

Simple changes.

Quiet discipline.

Walking.

Portion control.

Fasting.

Letting go of eating my emotions.

Learning to love myself back to life.

Eighty pounds later, I didn't just reclaim my body — I reclaimed my identity, my voice, my joy, and my peace.

This is my story.

Not of vanity, but of victory.

Not of perfection, but of persistence.

Not of weight loss, but of *Becoming Me Again*.

Chapter 1

Before the weight ever showed up on my body, life had already begun pressing its heaviness onto my spirit.

I grew up thin, active, carefree — a girl who ran everywhere instead of walking, who lived outside until the streetlights told her it was time to come home. Food wasn't a reward or a burden. It was simply what it was meant to be: nourishment. Life was movement, laughter, and natural confidence.

Back then, I didn't think about my body. I *lived* in it. I didn't stand in mirrors trying to figure out what needed to be fixed. I wasn't measuring myself against anyone else. I wasn't carrying emotional weight I didn't yet understand. Life was simple. And I was free.

But somewhere along the way — slowly, subtly, quietly — that freedom began to fade. I didn't have a traumatic childhood around food. I didn't struggle with weight as a teenager or a young woman. My relationship with food was healthy and uncomplicated, until life became complicated. And that is where my journey truly began.

My weight gain didn't come from genetics. It came from responsibilities. It came from heartbreak, pressure, exhaustion and from season of survival that never seemed to end.

I didn't even notice the shift. Stress was manageable.

Life was busy but tolerable. The extra snacks, the comfort meals, the late-night eating — they all felt harmless at first.

Until one day, they weren't.

Emotional eating sneaks in through the back door of your life. It becomes the thing you reach for when you don't have the words, the support, or the strength to process what you're carrying.

It whispers:

"You deserve this."

"You've had a long day."

"You need a break."

"No one understands, but this is here for you."

Food became:

- A reward after long days serving everyone else
- Silence between tears I cried alone
- Comfort when life disappointed me
- Numbing when I didn't want to feel
- A companion when loneliness settled in

I wasn't eating because I was hungry. I was eating because I was hurting.

Food became my coping mechanism — my way to soothe stress I didn't talk about, pain I didn't acknowledge, and needs I didn't express. As the emotional weight piled up, the physical weight followed.

People think weight gain starts on the outside. But for most women, it starts in the heart.

Before I ever gained a pound, I was accumulating:

- Expectations I couldn't meet
- Responsibilities I never set aside
- Emotional exhaustion I didn't know how to release.
- Pressure to remain strong, composed, capable and unbreakable.

I became the woman holding everything together: at work, at home, within my family, and in my relationships. I was reliable, steady, strong—even when I felt tired, overwhelmed, or silently falling apart. Yet, as I supported everyone around me, I gradually neglected my own needs. I learned to prioritize others at my own expense, to bury my own desires beneath a mountain of obligations, and to mask my struggles with a façade of being fine. I knew how to care deeply and endlessly, but I didn't know how to give myself the rest I needed.

It wasn't an overnight transformation. It unfolded in the quiet moments when I placed myself at the bottom of the list. It was in the times I silenced my own needs, in the years of giving without replenishment, and in the emotional storms I refused to acknowledge. I didn't wake up one day to find myself 80 pounds heavier; instead, I woke up to realize that I had become a stranger to myself.

The woman who once laughed easily now found joy less often. The woman who once moved with grace now moved hesitantly. The woman who once loved herself without effort now struggled to recognize her own reflection. It wasn't only the physical weight I carried; it was also the emotional burden on my soul.

Scripture Reflection

"Come to me, all you who are weary and burdened, and I will give you rest." — Matthew 11:28

Before God asks us to be strong, He asks us to come home to Him. Before He asks for discipline, He offers rest. Before He calls us to rise, He invites us to release. I didn't know it then, but this verse would become a quiet anchor in my journey.

— — —

A Prayer for the Woman I Used to Be

Lord,

Thank You for seeing the woman I was long before I saw myself again. Thank You for loving me through every season — even the ones where I forgot how to love myself.

Heal the emotional weight I have carried in silence. Help me release what was never meant to stay with me. Guide me back to the woman You created me to be.

Amen.

Reflection Questions

1. When did your relationship with food begin to change?
2. What emotions do you carry in silence?
3. In what areas of your life have you been putting yourself last?
4. What version of yourself do you miss — and why?

Affirmation

"I honor the woman I was, the woman I am, and the woman I am becoming."

Chapter 2

There are seasons when a woman doesn't shatter in a single, cinematic moment. She fractures in quiet places no one notices.

Not onstage. Not in a public collapse. But in the small surrenders: the unseen sacrifices, the long, gray days, the disappointments left unsaid, the giving that never stops.

My breaking wasn't sudden. It was incremental.

Each time I said yes when I wanted to say no. Each time I swallowed my tired and kept moving. Each time I pushed my own needs aside because someone else seemed to need me "more." Each time I promised myself, "I'll rest later."

Later never arrived.

For more than forty years, my life was service. My vocation, my calling, my daily rhythm — to help, guide, protect, solve, support. People brought me their burdens, and I made them mine.

I took pride in it. I did it well. But my heart never clocked out.

Service became habit. Habit became identity.

I knew how to show up. I knew how to be strong. I knew how to give, even when I was empty.

What I didn't know was how to give that strength back to myself. I poured — even when the cup was dry. Especially then.

Motherhood remains one of my deepest privileges. My daughter is my joy, my heartbeat, God's entrusted blessing.

Yet love carries weight of its own. We give more than we imagine. We stretch until the edges fray. We become the steady ground for others' lives. And sometimes, in loving fiercely, we fade into the obligations we hold.

I was everything to everyone... until I became nothing to myself.

Caregiving changes you in ways you never see coming. When you spend years choosing others over yourself, you learn a kind of strength that doesn't roar — it whispers. You become the steady hands, the late-night comfort, the quiet sacrifice that no one ever fully sees. And while your heart expands in the process, a part of you slowly fades into the background, waiting for the moment you'll finally choose you. The impact is deep: it teaches compassion, resilience, and unconditional love, but it also reminds you that pouring from an empty cup is a slow kind of breaking. Caregiving is holy work, but reclaiming yourself afterward is healing work — the kind you deserve just as much as anyone you've cared for.

The day I realized I was missing wasn't dramatic. No shouting, no crisis — only a quiet clarity. I sat alone and heard a whisper: "You're gone." Not physically. Not even wholly emotionally. But spiritually — the woman I used to know had slipped away beneath stress, exhaustion, numbing comforts, and hidden resentments. I wasn't choosing me. I wasn't prioritizing me. I wasn't loving me. I had stopped tending to the woman behind the roles, the titles, the duties. The most painful truth was this: I didn't remember how to care for her anymore.

The truth found me in the mirror. Not a passing look — a long, searching stare to find the woman I recognized. She wasn't there. What I saw instead: A woman carrying years of quiet load. A woman bone-weary and thin with fatigue. A woman who'd given away joy, energy, and confidence, piece by piece. A woman who held everyone else steady — but not herself. That glass became my truth-teller. I didn't like the reflection. I didn't like how I felt. The heaviness on my body was real — but the weight in my spirit was the real burden.

Before a pound shows on the scale, it settles in the heart:

Stress, unspoken disappointment, loneliness. unreleased hurt and carried burdens. The pressure of being "the strong one."

Emotional weight piles up silently — and one day it demands space.

My weight gain wasn't only about food. It was the life I was living:

- The stress I internalized
- The feelings I never voiced
- The love I forgot to give myself
- The rest I postponed
- The boundaries I failed to draw
- The responsibilities I kept alone
- The needs I silenced

The weight was not the enemy — it was the symptom.

Every woman has a breaking point. And sometimes the break is the beginning of rescue. For me there was no dramatic collapse — only a piercing thought: "If I don't save myself, I will lose myself." It shook me. It terrified me. It woke me.

I had one life, one body, one soul, one chance to choose differently. In that exhausted, fearful place, something small and stubborn whispered: Begin again.

Not tomorrow. Not when you're rested. Not when everything aligns. Begin now. Begin tired. Begin unsure. Begin afraid.

Just begin.

— — —

Scripture for This Season:

"Come to me, all you who are weary and burdened, and I will give you rest." — Matthew 11:28

I didn't see it at first, but God was guiding me back — gently, lovingly — through truth and weariness.

— — —

Reflection Before the Rise:

Before the breakthrough came the breakdown. Before healing came honesty. Before transformation came truth.

This season broke me — and readied me. It softened the soil of my soul so new life could take root.

I didn't know then that my comeback had already begun.

— — —

Chapter Prayer

Lord, Open my eyes when I'm slipping away. Give me the courage to stop, to breathe, to face what's true, and to choose myself. Lift the load I was never meant to bear. Teach me that rest is holy, renewal is possible, and rebirth is my rightful gift. Amen.

— — —

Reflection Questions:

1. When did you first notice yourself slipping away?

2. Which responsibilities or emotions have quietly drained your spirit?

3. What truth about your health or heart are you avoiding?

4. What would choosing yourself look like today?

— — —

Affirmation

"I honor my breaking — because it is leading me back to myself."

Chapter 3

Every woman has someone whose love shapes her long before she understands why. Someone whose presence becomes a compass, whose voice becomes an anchor, whose belief becomes a blueprint for the life she eventually grows into.

For me, that person was my Uncle Johnny Goodrum.

He wasn't just an uncle. He was my second Dad.

He was the *standard*—the steady hand, the gentle strength, the voice of truth wrapped in love. He was emotional safety before I even had the language to name it. His presence was the kind you didn't have to explain; you just felt it. A knowing. A warmth. A certainty that you were protected.

Growing up, Uncle Johnny pushed me in the ways that mattered most.

He didn't push me to be perfect—he pushed me to rise.

To believe in myself.

To walk in doors, I thought were too heavy.

To speak when I felt small.

To expect more from myself than the world expected of me.

Where other people saw who I was, he saw what I could be.

He always had.

Even before I did.

He had this way of cutting through nonsense without ever raising his voice. He was a man of few words, but when he spoke—*Lord, it stuck.* And it stuck because it always came from a place of love. Even his corrections were covered in compassion.

But the moment that changed my life—the moment that became the turning point in my journey—came in a conversation I never expected.

It was a regular day.

No dramatic music playing in the background.

No warning.

Just him... looking at me with eyes that had seen me through every stage of my life.

He said it softly, but the truth carried weight:

"You are too pretty to carry all that weight."

For a moment, I forgot how to breathe.

I felt exposed. Seen. Uncomfortable.

But not judged.

He wasn't talking about vanity.

He wasn't talking about looks.

He was talking about the light I had lost.

The sparkle that dimmed.

The heaviness I didn't even know was visible to the people who loved me.

Before I could even respond, he added something that pierced even deeper:

"I don't recognize you anymore."

There was no anger.

No shame.

No disappointment.

Just concern.

Just truth.

Just love.

I didn't cry in front of him.

I nodded. I smiled. I brushed it off like it was just another one of his tough-love comments.

But later that night, when the house was quiet and the weight of my life pressed against my chest, his words echoed over and over:

"I don't recognize you anymore."

Sometimes God sends the truth through someone you can't ignore. That moment didn't break me—it woke me up.

Because deep down, I didn't recognize myself either.

I had lost the woman I used to be.

The joy.

The energy.

The confidence.

The vibrance.

The fire.

The faith in myself.

His words became the mirror I had been avoiding.

The mirror I needed.

Life did what life does—it shifted in a painful direction. Dementia began slowly, quietly, and cruelly pulling pieces of him away. A little memory here. A little clarity there. A little sparkle dimmed. The man who had always been strong, sharp, unshakeable... began slipping into a world where I could not follow.

That's when a promise rose in my heart—one I didn't speak out loud, but I felt in my bones. I wanted him to see me again. Really see me. Before he transitioned. Not just a body changing... but a woman returning to herself.

I made a quiet vow:

I would lose the weight.

I would reclaim my life.

I would do the work.

And I would let him witness my becoming. God, in His perfect timing, honored that desire.

One of our last clear conversations—the last moment before dementia took him fully from us—became a gift I will carry for the rest of my life.

He noticed.

He saw the difference.

He smiled with pride.

He recognized me again.

And for a brief, sacred moment, I felt like we were back to who we had always been:

Just me and him.

Just "Kid" and Uncle Johnny. "

Just love.

Just truth.

Just us.

That moment stitched itself into the fabric of my healing.

It became a blessing over my transformation. It became a whisper from heaven: "Keep going."

Uncle Johnny wasn't just the catalyst for my weight loss—he was the embodiment of the love that reminded me who I was. His belief in me is woven into every step I took.

Into every pound I lost. Into every choice I made to return home to myself.

Even now, I hear him in my spirit:

"Yes, you can, Kid."

I still whisper back:

"Thank you for seeing me... before I saw myself again."

— — —

Reflection Questions:

1. Who in your life has spoken truth to you with love?

2. What moment or conversation awakened you to the change you needed?

3. What promise have you made to yourself—or someone you love—that deserves to be honored?

— — —

Affirmation

I welcome the voices of love, truth, and guidance. I am becoming the woman I was always meant to be.

— — —

Prayer

Lord, thank You for the people who speak truth into our lives with love and compassion. Thank You for the voices that guide us, uplift us, and awaken us to our purpose. Help me honor their influence by becoming the best version of myself. Strengthen me to walk boldly in transformation, healing, and discipline. Amen.

Chapter 4

"*Sometimes your glow returns before you even realize you're shining again.*"

There is a very specific kind of magic that happens when you begin to change — a quiet shift, a soft brightness, a subtle confidence that blooms around you before you even recognize it in yourself. That's what happened to me.

At first, the changes were small. My face looked a little slimmer. My walk felt a little lighter. My clothes fit a little differently. But even as my body slowly transformed, it was the world around me that reflected my progress back to me like a mirror I hadn't known I needed.

I remember the first time someone genuinely didn't recognize me. I walked into a store, waved at a woman I'd known for years, and she walked right past me with a polite smile — the kind you give a stranger. I spoke again, and her eyes widened like she'd seen a ghost.

"Wenomia? Oh, my goodness! Look at you!"

She stepped back to take me in the way people do when they're trying to piece together a before-and-after puzzle. Her reaction was so genuine, so heartfelt, that for a moment I felt emotional. Not because she saw the weight loss, but because she saw *me*.

That became a pattern. At work, coworkers whispered to each other, shocked at how quickly I seemed to be changing. Some stopped me in hallways. Others stared for a few seconds before the recognition hit.

Family gatherings turned into celebrations.

Church turned into encouragement sessions.

Social events turned into affirmations wrapped in hugs and wide smiles.

People saw strength in me before I fully claimed it. There is nothing quite like being both familiar and unrecognizable at the same time.

My voice was the same.

My laugh was the same.

My heart was the same.

But the woman they saw — the woman standing tall, smiling wider, and moving with ease — felt new to them, and sometimes even new to me.

I didn't realize how much of myself had been hidden behind the weight until it began to disappear. And it wasn't just physical visibility — it was emotional visibility. People weren't just seeing my body change; they were seeing *me* return.

The Positivity Was Overwhelming; in the best way. Every reaction was rooted in love, support, or genuine amazement.

Friends said, "You look like yourself again."

Coworkers said, "You're glowing."

Women whispered, "Tell me what you're doing."

Men looked twice, not out of vanity, but out of respect for the discipline they saw.

Family said, "We're so proud of you."

Not a single person responded with negativity or envy.

Not one.

The joy people had for me felt like fuel. Their pride in my journey became wind beneath my wings. Every compliment, every double-take, every word of encouragement was a reminder that my hard work was not invisible.

It took me a while to realize something. People weren't reacting to the weight I lost. They were reacting to the woman I was becoming.

They saw:

- My confidence returning
- My joy warming my face again
- My energy rising
- My posture lifting
- My spirit opening

They saw a woman who chose herself.

A woman who didn't give up. A woman walking with purpose again. They saw a light in me that had dimmed for too long — and they celebrated its return.

Human beings need witnesses. Not for validation, but for reflection. Sometimes you don't know how far you've come until someone else tells you.

The reactions I received became part of my healing. They reminded me that even though the journey felt slow and personal, the transformation was visible, powerful, and real.

In every person's eye, I saw a glimpse of the woman God was reshaping me into.

— — —

Scripture to Anchor This Chapter
"Arise, shine, for your light has come, and the glory of the Lord rises upon you." — Isaiah 60:1

— — —

Reflection Questions
1.   How do you typically respond to compliments or encouragement?
2.   What changes have others noticed in you before you noticed them yourself?
3.   How does it feel to be truly *seen* in your journey?
4.   What reactions uplift you the most — and why?

— — —

Affirmation
"I am becoming a woman whose light is impossible to ignore."

— — —

Prayer
Lord, thank You for surrounding me with people who see the beauty in my growth. Help me to receive their encouragement with humility and grace. Strengthen my spirit so I may continue to walk boldly in the transformation You have begun in me. May my journey reflect your goodness, and a testimony of what discipline, faith, and self-love can create. Amen.

Chapter 5

"*Before I ever carried weight on my body, I carried it in my heart.*"

There is a kind of heaviness a woman can wear that no one else can see. It doesn't show up on a scale. It doesn't rest on her hips or her waistline. It doesn't stretch her clothes or change her reflection — not at first.

Before my weight gain ever became visible to the world, it lived in my spirit. It was the quiet heaviness.

The kind that builds a little at a time. A whispered burden that becomes a familiar voice. I carried so much, long before my body ever did.

Women are taught — directly or indirectly — that we must be everything for everyone. We become the rock, the nurturer, the problem-solver, the caretaker, the glue holding everything together. And if we do it well enough, no one even realizes we're struggling.

I was praised for my strength. But no one asked about my exhaustion. People admired my reliability.

But no one saw how often I put myself last.

I carried:

- The expectations of family
- The expectations of motherhood
- The expectations of my career
- The expectations I placed on myself

Little by little, I became the woman who said "I'm fine" even when I wasn't.

Stress is sneaky. It doesn't always show up with loud alarms. Sometimes it arrives quietly — through long days, hard seasons, and responsibilities that pile up until you feel buried under them.

I lived in a constant state of doing. A constant state of giving.

A constant state of managing, helping, supporting, and solving. People needed me. And I answered every call.

But the weight of stress began to live in my body:

- In the tension in my shoulders
- In the knots in my stomach
- In the late-night snacking for comfort
- In the emotional overeating I didn't want to admit
- In the exhaustion that felt impossible to shake

Food became my pause button, my relief and my temporary escape. But what I didn't realize was that while I was soothing my stress, I was burying myself deeper inside it.

Heartbreak changes a woman. Not just romantic heartbreak — emotional heartbreak, family heartbreak, disappointment, betrayal, loneliness and grief.

There were seasons in my life when I felt unseen. Seasons when I poured into people who could not or would not pour back into me. Seasons when I prayed for peace but lived in storms. I didn't know how to voice some of the pain I was carrying, so I swallowed it. And swallowed it. And swallowed it. Until my body began showing the symptoms of what my heart had been feeling for years.

THE WEIGHT OF NOT FEELING GOOD ENOUGH

Self-doubt isn't loud. It whispers.

Women can accomplish everything — raise families, build careers, show up for loved ones, survive storms — and still wrestle with the inner voice that says:

"Is who I am... enough?"

I had moments where I questioned:

- My beauty
- My worth
- My importance
- My choices
- My identity beyond motherhood and work

I was giving the world love and strength — but giving myself judgment and neglect.

My emotional weight was the result of years of:

- Avoiding my own needs
- Ignoring my own pain
- Prioritizing everyone else
- Believing I could handle everything alone

But no woman can live like that forever. Eventually, the emotional weight demands to be dealt with.

My struggle wasn't food — it was what food meant to me.

I ate:

- When I was overwhelmed
- When I was lonely
- When I was stressed
- When I was sad
- When I was trying not to think
- When I was trying not to feel

Food became a friend I didn't have to explain myself to. A comfort that didn't ask questions. A reward I convinced myself I deserved. A relief I could always count on.

But emotional eating doesn't heal anything. It just delays the hurt. When the healing never comes...the weight does.

It's difficult to acknowledge the truth, and the hardest weight to lose is what you feel inside. I reached a point where I understood something I had avoided. I wasn't just carrying physical weight. I was carrying:

- Fear
- Disappointment
- Guilt
- Regret
- Shame
- Stress
- Unspoken hurt

Losing weight was not just about food, or discipline, or exercise.

It was about:

- Facing the woman I had avoided
- Accepting the emotions I had ignored
- Breaking patterns that no longer served me
- Learning to soothe my soul instead of my appetite
- Letting God into the places I had been trying to fix alone.

This chapter — this emotional chapter was the turning point of my entire journey. Because the truth is "It is impossible to release physical weight while clinging to emotional weight." One must go before the other.

The healing began with honesty. Healing didn't begin with a scale. It began with a mirror.

It began with the courage to say:

"I am hurting."

"I am overwhelmed."

"I am tired."

"I need help."

"I deserve better."

"I want to come back to myself."

I learned to:

- Name my stress
- Feel my emotions
- Forgive myself for coping the only way I knew how
- Replace old habits with healing ones
- Choose nourishment over numbing
- Let go of guilt
- Invite God into my weaknesses

The emotional work was difficult, but it was also necessary — and ultimately, it set me free.

— — —

SCRIPTURE THAT CARRIED ME

"Cast all your cares upon Him, for He cares for you." – 1 Peter 5:7

This verse became a lifeline. I didn't have to carry everything alone. I wasn't meant to. God wasn't asking me to be strong for everyone — He was asking me to let Him be strong for me.

— — —

REFLECTION QUESTIONS

1. What emotional weight have you been carrying in silence?

2. What expectations have you accepted that are draining you?

3. When was the last time you checked in with your own heart?

4. Do you use food to comfort emotions you don't want to feel?

5. What would healing look like for you right now?

— — —

PRAYER

Father,

Help me release the weight no one sees. Heal the wounds I buried, the stress I carried, the heartbreak I hid, and the expectations I never deserved to bear. Teach me to nourish my body and my soul. Guide me toward habits that honor the woman You created me to be. Lift the emotional burdens that have lived in me for too long. Restore my peace, renew my strength, and lead me gently back to myself.

Amen.

Chapter 6

Motivation started my journey, but it didn't sustain it.

Motivation is a spark — bright, exciting, emotional. It makes promises in the morning and disappears by nightfall. It gives us a rush, a feeling, a moment. But when life hits hard... when stress rises... when emotions flare... when old habits whisper... motivation goes silent.

Discipline, though —discipline shows up even when we don't feel like it.

For decades, I lived in a cycle familiar to so many women.

I would get motivated, start strong, make changes, then fall off track the moment life shifted. One stressful week, one emotional day, one disappointment, one moment of exhaustion — that's all it took.

Motivation made me *want* change.

Discipline helped me *become* changed.

It wasn't until I embraced discipline that everything in my journey transformed.

— — —

The Day I Realized Motivation Wasn't Enough

There was a morning when I woke up and felt that "nothing" feeling — the heaviness that makes you want to pull the covers back over your head. I didn't want to walk. I didn't want to measure my portions. I didn't want to think about habits or progress or goals.

Motivation was nowhere to be found.

But something whispered inside me:

"Do it anyway."

So I did.

I got up.

I walked.

I kept my promise to myself.

And afterward — I felt strong.

That moment taught me that discipline wasn't punishment.

It was love.

It was protection.

It was me choosing me — even when I didn't feel like it.

— — —

The Power of Daily Routines

Once discipline became my foundation, everything shifted.

Routines became anchors — steady, dependable, grounding.

I didn't overhaul my life overnight.

I built it step by step:

• Nourishing meals instead of emotional meals

Food became intentional again — a way to fuel my body, not numb my feelings.

• Drinking more water even when I preferred comfort drinks

My body thanked me. My skin thanked me. My energy thanked me.

• Moving daily, not perfectly

Some days I walked long.

Some days I walked slow.

Some days I just kept the promise to move.

• Creating bedtime rhythms that honored my rest

Rest became a spiritual practice — a way to quiet my mind and honor God's design for my body.

• Protecting my energy with boundaries

Some people didn't understand, and that was okay.

I was no longer living in a world where everyone else came first.

• Managing stress before it managed me

Deep breaths.

Journaling.

Prayer.

Silence.

Self-awareness.

• Practicing affirmations and gratitude

I learned to speak life into myself instead of waiting for others to do it.

These weren't rules.

These were acts of devotion to myself.

Discipline became my daily "I love you."

— — —

When Discipline Became My Love Language

The more disciplined I became, the more I realized something sacred:

Discipline is a form of self-respect.

Self-respect builds confidence.

Confidence builds identity.

Identity builds freedom.

This wasn't about weight loss anymore.

This was about reclaiming my life.

Every healthy choice — big or small — was a declaration:

"I deserve this.

I am worthy of care.

I am worthy of effort.

I am worthy of consistency."

Even on the hard days.

Especially on the hard days.

— — —

Discipline Made Me Emotionally Stronger

Something unexpected happened as I grew more disciplined:

I stopped being so easily shaken.

I became steadier.

Clearer.

More grounded.

Less reactive.

More patient.

More connected to myself and to God.

Discipline built a strength in me that weight loss alone never could.

It became the quiet confidence that whispers,

"You can do this,"

even when the world feels heavy.

— — —

What Discipline Really Means

Discipline is not strictness.

It is not suffering.

It is not deprivation.

Discipline is choosing your future self over your current feelings.

It is honoring the woman you're becoming — not just the woman you currently are.

It is trusting that showing up for yourself today will bless you tomorrow.

And the greatest lesson of all?

Discipline is a spiritual act.

Every time I honored my body...

Every time I said no to old habits...

Every time I pushed through...

Every time I stayed consistent...

I was telling God:

"Thank You for this body. I will take care of it."

— — —

Scripture to Carry With You

"No discipline seems pleasant at the time, but painful. Later, however, it produces a harvest of righteousness and peace."

— Hebrews 12:11 (NIV)

This scripture became real to me.

Hard at first.

Harvest later.

Peace always.

— — —

Reflection Questions

1. When have you relied on motivation instead of discipline?

2. What small daily routine could anchor your life right now?

3. What is one habit that your future self will thank you for?

4. How can you protect your peace with boundaries this week?

5. Which area of your life needs consistent love — not occasional effort?

— — —

Affirmation

"I am committed to the woman I am becoming.

My discipline is my strength, my protection, and my promise to myself."

— — —

Prayer

Lord, help me honor this body, this life, and this journey.

Teach me discipline that is rooted in love — not fear, not pressure, not perfection.

Strengthen me on days when motivation fades.

Guide my habits, my choices, and my daily steps.

Let every act of consistency draw me closer to the healthiest, happiest, most whole version of myself.

Amen.

Chapter 7

Transformation is not a straight line. It is not neat or predictable or easy. It is a winding road of progress, pauses, stumbles, and grace.

My journey was no different.

People often see the "after," but they rarely see the middle — the messy middle where doubt creeps in, discipline wavers, and the old version of you tries to pull you back. My setbacks weren't failures. They were teachers. Even though they hurt, they grew me. Even though they slowed me down, they shaped me.

But let me be honest:

There were days I didn't want to keep going.

Days when the scale refused to move, and days when it moved backward. Days when emotional eating tried to reclaim me. Days when stress stretched me thin. Days when loneliness whispered old lies. Days when life felt heavy and progress felt impossible.

And still... I kept going.

— — —

The Unexpected Weight of Plateaus

The first time I hit a plateau, I felt defeated. I had been working so hard — walking, fasting, being intentional — and suddenly the scale wouldn't budge. I questioned myself:

"Am I doing something wrong?"

"Why isn't this working anymore?"

"Maybe this is just how my body is now."

Plateaus are silent discouragers. They test your patience and your faith. They make you wonder if all the effort is even worth it. But I learned something powerful: A plateau is not punishment. It is preparation.

God was teaching me endurance. He was teaching me trust.

He was teaching me to separate my progress from a number on a scale. Sometimes your body pauses so your mind and spirit can catch up to who you're becoming.

— — —

Setbacks That Tried to Steal My Progress

I faced setbacks that came suddenly and setbacks that crept in slowly.

Holidays and Emotional Triggers

Food has a way of calling your name when life gets stressful or lonely.

Holidays were especially hard — the smells, the traditions, the emotional connection to meals. Old habits tried to pull me backward.

But I reminded myself:

One bad day is not a bad journey.

Stress That Silenced My Discipline

There were days when the emotional load was too heavy and discipline felt far away. When you're tired or hurting, food can feel like the easiest comfort. I slipped more than once. I lost focus more than once. But each time I reminded myself:

Grace over guilt. Progress over perfection.

Moments I Wanted to Quit

I had moments when quitting felt easier than continuing — moments when I thought, *"Maybe this is just who I am now."*

But then I remembered the woman I wanted to become.

I remembered my "why."

I remembered Uncle Johnny's words.

I remembered that I had already survived harder things in life than a setback.

— — —

Why I Didn't Quit

I didn't quit because...

1. I Was Tired of Starting Over

Every time I restarted in the past, it was because I had quit.

I made a decision on this journey: I will not quit on myself again. If I slipped, I got back up the next day — sometimes the next hour. Restarting wasn't failure. It was strength.

2. I Learned That Discipline Protects You

Discipline became my anchor. Not motivation.

Motivation is emotional — it fades when life gets hard.

Discipline is spiritual — it holds you steady.

On the days I didn't feel like doing anything, discipline whispered: *"Just take one step."*

3. I Began to Love the Woman I Was Becoming

Once you get a taste of your own growth, it becomes harder to return to who you used to be. Every small win, every pound lost, every shift in my mindset reminded me that quitting would not only betray my body — it would betray my purpose.

4. I Realized Setbacks Are Part of Success

There is no transformation without resistance.

There is no breakthrough without pressure.

There is no strength without struggle.

Setbacks were not signs to stop — they were signs that I was growing.

— — —

The Moment Everything Shifted

The moment I truly changed was not when I lost the first pound, or the tenth, or even the fiftieth.

The real transformation happened the day I said:

"I am not quitting this time."

Something spiritual unlocked inside me.

I stopped being afraid of going slow.

I only feared going backward.

And even on my worst days, I kept one promise to myself:

Keep showing up.

Some days I showed up big.

Some days I showed up small.

But I showed up.

Because healing is not in perfection — it is in presence.

— — —

Reflection: What Setbacks Taught Me

Looking back, I'm grateful for every setback, because they taught me:

- Resilience is built, not born.
- Consistency matters more than intensity.
- Grace is a requirement, not a reward.
- The journey is emotional before it is physical.
- You don't lose just because you struggle. You lose when you stop trying.

My setbacks didn't stop me.

They strengthened me.

They helped shape the woman I am today — a woman who doesn't quit on herself.

— — —

Scripture for Strength

Galatians 6:9 (NIV)

"Let us not become weary in doing good, for at the proper time we will reap a harvest if we do not give up."

— — —

Prayer

Lord, strengthen me when I grow weary.

Help me see setbacks not as failures, but as lessons.

Remind me that You walk beside me even on the hardest days. Give me discipline where motivation is missing,

and remind me that progress is still progress,

even when it feels slow. Thank You for the resilience You are building in me.

Amen.

— — —

Reflection Questions:

1.   When you face setbacks, what thoughts or emotions rise first?

2.   What is your "why" — the reason you won't quit this time?

3.   Which setback has taught you the most about yourself?

4.   What small promise can you make to yourself today to keep going?

Chapter 8

There is a moment in every transformation when the outside finally begins to match the inside. A moment when the mirror becomes a friend again — not a reminder of who you used to be, but a celebration of who you fought to become. For me, that moment arrived slowly, then all at once.

Eighty pounds later, I didn't just see a new body.

I saw a resurrected spirit.

For so long, I walked through life heavy — physically, emotionally, mentally. My steps were slower. My breath was shorter. My confidence was smaller. My world felt dimmer. But now, each morning that I wake up, I rise with a different energy. A different light. A different presence.

I walk in a version of myself that once felt unreachable.

Not because I lacked desire.

But because I lacked belief.

And belief is the birthplace of every transformation.

— — —

The Woman in the Mirror

The first time I recognized myself again, it wasn't because of a number on a scale. It was because of a feeling — a quiet, steady confidence rising inside me.

I saw:

- A woman who kept showing up
- A woman who didn't quit on herself
- A woman who honored her promise
- A woman who broke generational habits
- A woman who rebuilt her relationship with her body
- A woman who chose discipline over doubt
- A woman who remembered her own worth

The mirror stopped being something I avoided and became something I appreciated. Not for vanity, but for validation — proof of the internal work manifested in physical form.

— — —

The Way My Body Feels Now

Eighty pounds later, everything feels different.

My breathing is deeper.

My movements are easier.

My sleep is richer.

My energy is stronger.

My posture is taller.

My smile is wider.

I walk with purpose.

I move with intention.

I speak with conviction.

I live with gratitude.

There is a freedom I never knew I needed until I experienced it.

Freedom in my clothes.

Freedom in my body.

Freedom in my emotions.

Freedom in my mind.

Freedom in my spirit.

Losing weight gave me room to breathe — but gaining myself back gave me room to live.

— — —

The Confidence I Thought Was Gone Forever

There is a unique kind of confidence that comes from discipline.

From knowing you kept going.

From seeing your own resilience in motion.

I didn't buy this confidence.

I built it.

Every walk.

Every meal choice.

Every "no" to old habits.

Every "yes" to myself.

Every restart.

Every prayer.

Every tear.

Every victory.

Confidence didn't arrive at the end of the journey — it was built piece by piece along the way.

I no longer shrink.

I no longer apologize for taking up space.

I no longer silence my needs.

I no longer hide in the back of photos.

I am not a new woman — I am simply the woman I was always meant to be, finally given room to rise.

— — —

What Peace Feels Like Now

There were years when peace felt like a luxury I couldn't afford.

Now, peace is the foundation of my life.

Peace in my routines.

Peace in my boundaries.

Peace in my body.

Peace in my decisions.

Peace in my identity.

I didn't just lose weight — I released what was weighing down my spirit.

Stress that used to overwhelm me became easier to manage.

Heartbreaks that once crushed me grew smaller in the shadow of my healing.

Expectations that drained me no longer hold power over my worth.

Peace is the quiet reward of choosing yourself.

— — —

The Spiritual Shift

Transformation is not just physical — it's spiritual.

God met me in the moments when I felt the weakest.

When I prayed for strength to keep going.

When I cried over the weight — not just on my body, but on my heart.

When I felt alone, lost, or exhausted.

And through every moment of discipline, I found myself drawing closer to Him.

I realized something profound:

God never required perfection from me — only effort.

He didn't ask me to be flawless — only faithful.

And every step I took toward a healthier version of myself was a step back toward Him.

— — —

The Joy I Carry Now

Joy looks different on me now.

It's not loud or forced — it's steady and rooted.

Joy shows up in the way I laugh without self-consciousness.

In the way I walk into a room without shrinking.

In the way I take photos without hiding.

In the way I honor my boundaries.

In the way I nourish my body with gratitude.

Joy is the glow that happens when a woman returns home to herself.

— — —

The Pride I Feel in My Journey

I used to think pride was about the final result.

Now I know pride is about the journey.

I am proud of:

- The woman who started
- The woman who struggled

- The woman who kept going
- The woman who broke cycles
- The woman who healed
- The woman who prayed through it
- The woman who didn't quit

Eighty pounds later, I know this truth:

My body changed because I changed.

My spirit rose because I rose.

My life transformed because I chose me.

— — —

A Prayer of Gratitude

Dear God,

Thank You for guiding me back to myself. Thank You for the strength to change, the courage to continue, and the grace to grow. Thank You for every lesson, every tear, every victory.

Let my story inspire others to believe in their own rebirth.

May my journey honor You, and may my life reflect the woman You always saw in me.

Amen.

Chapter 9

Transformation doesn't happen in one big moment. It happens in the quiet ones — the ones no one sees. The mornings you choose water over soda. The evenings you walk instead of sitting in the heaviness of the day. The days you show up for yourself even when motivation is nowhere to be found.

By the time I lost 80 pounds, I had learned something simple and life changing. The journey isn't about the weight you lose. It's about the woman you discover along the way.

Losing weight changed my body, yes — but the biggest shift happened in my mind, my habits, my confidence, my faith, and my understanding of myself. I learned what I needed, what I deserved, and who I truly was beneath the layers of emotional and physical heaviness.

And I learned that anyone — no matter how far off track they feel — can begin the same way I did:

with one small step.

— — —

THE LESSONS THAT REBUILT ME

These are the truths that reshaped my life one day, one choice, one breath at a time.

1. Small Steps Matter More Than Perfect Plans

For years, I believed change had to be dramatic — a strict diet, an intense workout plan, a complete overhaul. But the real transformation happened in small acts of discipline:

A 10-minute walk.

Choosing baked over fried.

Drinking one extra bottle of water.

Saying *no* when I was overwhelmed.

Going to bed instead of stress-eating.

The small steps I took daily created a momentum that changed everything.

God honors small beginnings — not perfect performances.

— — —

2. Your Pace Is Your Power

I wasn't in competition with anyone. My journey wasn't meant to look like anybody else's.

Some weeks I lost weight.

Some weeks nothing changed.

Some weeks I gained.

But I learned that slow progress is still progress. God was never asking me to be fast — He was asking me to be faithful.

— —

3. Grace Is More Important Than Guilt

Guilt keeps you stuck.

Grace sets you free.

When I slipped up, I didn't let it turn into a bad week, a bad month, or a complete abandonment of my goals.

I gave myself grace.

I prayed.

I started again.

Grace gave me the strength to continue.

Guilt only ever made me want to quit.

— — —

4. Water, Rest, Stress, and Boundaries Matter More Than Diets

I used to think weight loss was only about food.

But healing taught me it was about:

- Drinking enough water to clear my mind and body
- Sleeping enough to think clearly
- Managing stress before it drove me back to emotional eating
- Setting boundaries so I didn't carry weight that wasn't mine

These lifestyle changes mattered more than any meal plan I ever followed.

— — —

5. Consistency Beats Motivation Every Time

Motivation comes and goes.

Some mornings I was unstoppable.

Some mornings I didn't want to move.

But discipline — quiet, steady, consistent discipline — carried me through the days when motivation was nowhere to be found.

Discipline said:

"Even if you don't feel like it, do something."

And something was always enough.

— — —

6. You Are Allowed to Choose Yourself

This was the hardest and most beautiful lesson.

As women, we often feel guilty prioritizing ourselves.

But choosing yourself isn't selfish — it's survival.

I learned that I could love others deeply *and* love myself well.

I could show up for people without disappearing in the process.

I could give from a place of fullness instead of exhaustion.

Choosing myself didn't make me less loving — it made me whole.

— — —

HOW YOU CAN START TODAY

You don't need to wait for a new week, a perfect moment, or a fresh season.

You can start today — right now — with the smallest, simplest step.

Try one of these:

1. Drink more water.

Your body will thank you.

2. Walk for 10–20 minutes.

Movement clears the mind and strengthens the spirit.

3. Add vegetables to one meal.

Small nutritional changes accumulate.

4. Write your goals down.

Clarity creates direction.

5. Track your habits.

Awareness leads to transformation.

6. Celebrate every win.

No victory is too small.

7. Restart as many times as you need.

There is no shame in beginning again.

— — —

JOURNALING PROMPTS FOR BECOMING

These prompts are invitations to look inward and speak truth into your journey.

· What does "becoming me again" mean in this season of your life?

· Which habits, relationships, or patterns no longer serve the woman you're becoming?

· What version of yourself are you ready to meet?

· What would your healthiest, happiest self-thank you for today?

· What emotional weight do you need to release?

· What boundaries do you need to set to protect your peace?

— — —

DAILY AFFIRMATIONS FOR SELF-LOVE AND DISCIPLINE

Speak these until you believe them:

- I am becoming the best version of myself.
- I choose discipline over doubt.
- I release what no longer serves me.
- I am worthy of a healthy, joyful life.
- I honor my body, my mind, and my spirit.
- I show up for myself every day.

Affirmations are seeds — speak them, water them, and watch them grow.

— — —

A PRAYER FOR YOUR JOURNEY
Father,
Thank You for the strength to begin again.
Thank You for seeing the woman I am becoming, even on the days I can't see her myself.
Give me discipline when I am distracted,
grace when I fall short,
and courage when I feel afraid.
Release the weight I carry in my heart,
and guide me toward healing, peace, and purpose.
Walk with me as I choose myself,
one small step at a time.
Amen.

— — —

SCRIPTURE
Galatians 6:9 (NIV)
"Let us not become weary in doing good, for at the proper time we will reap a harvest if we do not give up."
A reminder:

Nothing is wasted.
Nothing is too late.
Your harvest is coming.

Chapter 10

To the woman holding this book in her hands — yes, you.

Maybe you whispered to yourself, *"Something has to change."* Maybe you turned a page hoping to feel understood. Maybe you're tired of starting over. Maybe you feel forgotten, stretched thin, overwhelmed, or silently breaking.

Or maybe...

you're standing at the edge of your own comeback, unsure of how to begin.

Wherever you are, however, you feel, let me tell you this with all the love and honesty in my heart:

Your journey is sacred.

Your healing is possible.

And your becoming has already begun.

I know what it is to lose yourself slowly — so slowly you don't even notice until one day you wake up and ask, "Where am I? What happened to me?" I know what it feels like to pour into others while running on empty, to smile while wounded, to hold up the world while your knees shake underneath you.

But I also know what it feels like to rise.

Not all at once... but moment by moment.

Choice by choice.

Step by step.

Grace by grace.

And that same rising is waiting for you.

— — —

You Are Not Late

Women carry a quiet fear — that they've waited too long to change, too long to heal, too long to choose themselves. But let me free you from that lie:

You are not late.

You are right on time for your breakthrough, right on time for your healing, right on time for the version of yourself you've been longing to meet.

Transformation does not have an age limit.

Healing does not expire.

Self-love is never too late.

You can begin today.

You can begin now.

You can begin in the middle of your chaos, your grief, your loneliness, your frustration, your uncertainty.

You do not need perfect conditions — you just need permission.

And I am giving you that permission today.

— — —

You Are Not Broken

Life has a way of convincing us that our struggles are evidence of failure — but I want you to hear me:

You are not broken.

You are a woman who survived things she doesn't talk about.

You are a woman who kept going on days she wanted to quit.

You are a woman who holds her family, her home, her community together even when she feels like falling apart.

You are a woman who silently battles storms that would have drowned others.

Your exhaustion is not weakness.

Your weariness is not shameful.

Your vulnerability is not failure.

It is proof that you are human — and that you are still here.

— — —

You Are Not Unworthy

This journey — of healing, health, discipline, peace, joy — is not for "other women."

It is for you.

You are worthy of becoming the woman you dream about.

You are worthy of:

- a body that feels alive
- a mind that feels clear
- a heart that feels whole
- a life that feels joyful

You are worthy of rest, nourishment, boundaries, love, softness, and care.

The world has taken from you, drained you, pulled on you — but you deserve to receive.

You deserve to be cared for, honored, and poured into.

And the first person who gets to pour into you... is you.

— — —

Your Journey Back to Yourself will Not Look Like Mine —
and That's Okay

Your pace is holy.

Your steps are valid.

Your process is your own.

Some days you will feel unstoppable.

Other days you may feel discouraged.

Some days the scale will move.

Other days your healing will be invisible but just as real.

But hear me:

Every step toward yourself counts.

Every restart is strength.

Every small victory is a promise of who you are becoming.

Do not rush.

Do not compare.

Do not judge your progress by someone else's highlight reel.

God is writing *your* story — uniquely, intentionally, beauti-
fully.

— — —

You Will Rise — And You Already Are

Even reading this book is evidence that something inside you
is awakening.

A desire.

A hope.

A longing.

A quiet fire.

A whisper that says, *"I want my life back."*

That whisper is not accidental.

That whisper is God saying, *"Daughter, it's your time."*

You are rising even now — in the decision to begin, in the courage to face yourself, in the honesty to admit you want more.

Your rising does not need to be perfect.

Your rising does not need to be fast.

Your rising simply needs to be yours.

And when you look back, months from now, you will see a woman who refused to stay where she was.

A woman who chose herself even while shaking.

A woman who believed in her own comeback.

A woman who did not quit — not this time.

— — —

A Final Love Letter from Me to You

If no one has told you today, let me tell you:

You are strong.

You are beautiful.

You are capable.

You are worthy.

You are chosen.

You are becoming.

This book is my heart on paper — but it is also a mirror, reflecting at you the woman you can still become.

So, take a deep breath.

Place your hand on your heart.

Feel it beating beneath your palm.

That is your purpose.

That is your hope.

That is your proof that you still have time.

Your journey back to yourself begins now.

And I am rooting for you — every single step of the way.

With all my love and truth,

Wenomia

"You owe yourself the love that you so easily give to others."

Epilogue

I once believed healing was the destination.
   That if I could survive the breaking, endure the unraveling, and stitch myself back together, I would finally arrive.
   But healing, I've learned, is not an ending.
   It is a threshold.

   Becoming Me Again was never about returning to who I used to be.
   It was about remembering who I was before I learned to disappear, compromise my voice, or confuse love with endurance.
   This book ends here—but my becoming does not.

   What waits on the other side of healing is not perfection.
   It is recognition.
   It is peace that doesn't require explanation.
   It is love that doesn't wound in order to stay.

I am learning what it means to be met without shrinking.
To be chosen without being tested.
To rest without fear that rest will be taken away.

That story—the one that begins after the healing—
is already unfolding.
And when the time is right,
I will tell it.

For now, this is enough.
I am whole.
I am home.
I am becoming—still.

www.ingramcontent.com/pod-product-compliance
Lightning Source LLC
Chambersburg PA
CBHW020336130626
46549CB00003B/1195